Theses on the evolution of computer technology and its influence on our lives.

by Andreas Luck

Theses on the evolution of computer technology and its influence on our lives.

Dedicated to Annabelle T.

by Andreas Luck

Introduction:

We don't want to spend too much time here dealing with the past and present, which we all know well enough has already happened and can no longer be changed. Rather, in this paper we want to take a look into the near and distant future. I use my 40 years of experience in the fields of computer technology and all other media technologies as a basis. The recent past has proven me right again and again, that almost all of my forecasts and predictions have come true.

Table of contents:

Introduction	2
Past	5
Present & Future	6
Development of the components of computer technology	10
Intentional obsolescence	17
At home	19
TV technology	20
Smart urban planning	24
Landscape architecture	25
Cooking	27
Our jobs	33
Shopping of the future	36
Clothing	37
Sound engineering	39
Print media	41
Film production and the entertainment industry	45
Waste avoidance and recycling	46
Nursing & Medicine	49
The issue of life expectancy	53
Transport systems	55
The education system	65
Power supply	69
Development of space travel	72
Conclusions	80

The past:

The first ones were just as monstrous mechanical computer.

The evolution of computer technology has undergone an amazing development in the last hundred years. From the earliest mechanical calculators to the powerful, connected devices we see today, the computing landscape has changed rapidly. In this text we take a look at the milestones in computer technology, look at the current state of affairs and venture a glimpse into the future.

The beginnings of computer technology go back to the 20th century when inventors like Konrad Zuse developed groundbreaking concepts for mechanical calculating machines. These early devices, while rudimentary, laid the groundwork for automating computations.

A milestone in the history of computer technology was the invention of the first working computer, the ENIAC, in the 1940s. The ENIAC was a massive contraption that offered enormous computing power but required space for an entire room. In the decades that followed, computers became smaller, faster, and more powerful.

In the 1970s, the introduction of the microprocessor led to a revolution in computer technology. Suddenly, computers were no longer limited to large corporations or research institutions but became

accessible for general use. Companies like Apple and Microsoft released affordable personal computers that gained widespread acceptance and drove computerization into homes and offices.
The next few decades were characterized by ever smaller and more powerful computers. The introduction of laptops enabled increased mobility, while the development of smartphones revolutionized the entire technology landscape. Smartphones became small, versatile devices that not only enabled telephone calls but also functioned as cameras, music players, navigation devices and Internet access.
Computer networks also developed in parallel with the miniaturization of devices. The advent of the Internet in the 1990s led to a global interconnection of computers, enabling the seamless exchange of information and the emergence of new technologies such as cloud computing and artificial intelligence.

The presence:
Today we are in the age of the Internet of Things (IoT), where more and more devices are connected and able to exchange data. Smart homes, autonomous vehicles, and wearables are just a few examples of how computing technology is increasingly merging into our everyday lives.
But now to our actual main topic.

The future:

What does the future bring now? It can be expected that the development of computer technology will continue to make rapid progress. Artificial intelligence and machine learning are becoming more sophisticated, enabling new applications in areas such as healthcare, robotics, and automation. Quantum computing technology is

on the verge of a breakthrough and could revolutionize complex calculations.
In 1983, I already had the vision of computers that are only as big as a pack of cigarettes. As we all know, technology has moved in this direction and, with small deviations in mass, has arrived exactly the same way.

That's pretty much what my vision was like
Monitor glasses in 1986.

Then in 1986 I was inspired by a movie and made a different prediction. I had the vision that nowadays people wear semi-transparent glasses in which the glasses serve as a monitor, receive a signal via Wifi from the smartphone computer and are completely voice-controlled. Unfortunately, this technology was poorly implemented by Google and has not been continued.
Like the science fiction movies of the '90s, many movies used holographic monitor displays. I am firmly convinced that the monitor and flat screen will be replaced by a 3-dimensional holographic projection system shortly.

Holographic 3D Monitor Beam.

The storage media from the floppy to the mechanical HDD and then to the SSD are only the beginning. I am firmly convinced that in the near future new media such as living cells will be evolved from storage space, which will then have storage capacities of several zettabytes or even yottabytes. This development, as well as the development of ever more powerful processors, will also take place with the help of artificial intelligence, which of course also greatly increases the risk of misuse. Therefore, it is also our responsibility to always keep full control over the technology.

We remember that in the 1990s there were many Hollywood films in which artificial intelligence took over people and often wiped them out. We can already see that these are not pipe dreams by the fact that many visions from science fiction films, such as the proton or warp drive, are in the infancy of development today. It is always up to humanity and the people themselves which direction we take. How much this is the case can be seen again and again in dictatorships and totalitarian regimes that use our sophisticated technology to control, oppress and restrict people.

As early as 1973, work was being done in Germany on the development of what is known as a smart house, and it has been continuously developed further.
This technology is very exciting as it will significantly change the way people are cared for, safety, and comfort, among other things.
Now you will ask yourselves where I take and make all these predictions from. On the one hand from my experience in the I.T. sector, close observation of developments, analysis of what is feasible, and, of course, films. As a "child of the '80s", one likes to remember the futuristic imaginative science fiction. Some of it has already come true.

Nevertheless, there are still many challenges that we absolutely must solve:

Environmental degradation and climate change: careless use of natural resources, deforestation e.g. rainforests, air, water and soil pollution, and high emissions of greenhouse gases lead to a destabilized environment and climate change. Climate change has far-reaching effects on the ecosystem and poses a threat to the livelihoods of future generations.

Inequality and poverty: Despite progress in many areas, there are still major disparities in income, education, access to health care, and basic resources between different parts of the world's population. Poverty and inequality remain pressing problems that need to be overcome.

Conflicts and violence: Unfortunately, wars, terrorism, and armed conflicts are still a reality in many regions of the world. These conflicts cause great human suffering and prevent progress and development.

Lack of sustainability: In many areas, such as agriculture, energy production, and industry, too little value is placed on sustainability and environmental protection because there are some mega-corporations that still only care about their profits and the profits of their company shareholders think. This short-term thinking and pursuit of profit can lead to long-term damage.

Technological Challenges: Rapid technological advances bring both benefits and risks. The impact of artificial intelligence, automation, data breaches, and privacy are issues society must address to ensure technology is used for the good of humanity.

The development of the components of computer technology:

Futuristic mini high-performance computer

CPU processor technology is expected to evolve and undergo some important changes in the coming years. Here are some possible developments we might see in the CPU processor space in the future:

Multi-Core Processors: Multi-core processors are already widespread and this trend is expected to continue. Future CPUs may have a higher number of cores to further improve computing power. This allows for more efficient parallel processing of tasks and better performance when multitasking.

Coming light speed into computer technology.

Advances in Microarchitecture: Processor microarchitectures are expected to continue to improve to achieve higher performance while consuming less power. This can be achieved by optimizing pipelines, caches, instruction sets, and other processor structures.

Advances in Energy Efficiency: Efficiency is an important goal for future CPU processors. New technologies are expected to be developed to further reduce energy consumption, such as more advanced power-saving modes, better voltage regulation, and intelligent power management techniques.

Integrated graphics processors (GPUs): The integration of graphics processors in the CPUs is expected to continue to increase. This enables better graphics performance and accelerated processing of tasks that benefit from graphics-intensive applications such as gaming, video editing, and machine learning.

Memory hierarchy and cache technology: The memory hierarchy within CPUs could evolve to make accessing data more efficient. This can include the integration of larger caches, optimized memory access mechanisms, and new memory technologies such as persistent disks (e.g. Intel Optane).

Quantum Computing: Quantum computing is an emerging field that is very different from traditional processors. Although quantum processors are still in their infancy, in the future they could offer new approaches to solving complex problems that are difficult for conventional processors to solve.

This is what quantum processors could look like.

It is important to note that the precise direction and specific technologies employed in CPU processor technology will depend on various factors such as research and development, demand, economic considerations and technological breakthroughs.

Storage Media: Computer storage technology is constantly evolving to meet increasing demands for capacity, speed, and reliability. Here are some possible changes we might see in computer memory technology in the future:

Solid-State Drives (SSDs): SSDs have already replaced traditional hard disk drives (HDDs) in many areas because they are faster, quieter and more reliable. The capacity of SSDs is expected to continue increasing while prices fall. Advances in NAND flash memory technology, such as the introduction of 3D NAND and QLC (quad-level cell), enable higher storage capacities per chip.

Non-Volatile Memory: Research and development are focused on developing non-volatile memory that can store data without power. Technologies such as resistive RAM (RRAM), phase change memory (PCM), spintronics, and magneto resistive random access memory (MRAM) could play a bigger role in the future and offer higher memory density, faster access times, and better energy efficiency.

Futuristic optical storage.

Optical storage: Optical storage technologies could experience a renaissance in the future. With advances in holographic data storage and the use of laser technology, optical storage media could offer greater capacity and longer lifespans. The development of 5D memories on nanostructured glass media also shows promising approaches.

Cloud storage: The trend toward cloud usage is expected to continue, which means that more and more data will be stored in decentralized data centers. Cloud providers will continue to invest in expanding their storage capacities to meet the increasing need for data storage and processing.

Quantum memory: In the field of quantum computing, work is also being done on the development of quantum memories. These storage technologies could make it possible to store quantum bits (qubits) for longer periods, thereby improving the scalability and reliability of quantum computers.

It is important to note that the precise direction and specific technologies in storage engineering will depend on various factors such as research and development, economic considerations, and technological breakthroughs. However, the continued demand for higher capacity, speed, and efficiency will undoubtedly drive further advances in storage technology.

Laptops: In the future, laptops are expected to evolve and introduce new technologies to improve usability, performance, and portability. Here are some possible changes we might see in laptop technology in the future:

Improved performance: Future laptops are expected to use more powerful processors, graphics chips, and storage technologies to better handle compute-intensive tasks and demanding applications. This allows for seamless multitasking, faster data processing, and improved graphics performance.

Flexible displays: The development of flexible display technologies, such as e.g. B. OLED or Micro-LED could lead to laptops with bendable or rollable screens coming onto the market. This would increase flexibility and mobility and potentially allow for new form factors.

Lighter and Thinner: Advances in material technology and manufacturing techniques could lead to lighter and thinner laptops without compromising on performance. This would increase mobility and convenience, allowing users to easily take their laptops with them wherever they go.

Longer battery life: Improving the energy efficiency of components and developing more powerful batteries could result in longer battery life. This would allow users to use their laptops longer without charging and further improve mobility.

Expanded Connectivity: Future laptops could have expanded connectivity features, including the integration of 5G or even 6G connectivity to allow for faster wireless connections and greater access to cloud services. This would enable seamless communication and access to online resources in real-time.

Enhanced Security: Laptop security is expected to continue to improve to counter the rising cybercrime threats. This can include integrating biometric authentication methods such as fingerprint or face recognition systems, as well as improving encryption technologies.

Evolution of Smartphones:

Here are some possible changes we might see in smartphone technology in the future:

Foldable displays: Foldable smartphones are already on the market and this technology is expected to continue to evolve.
Here I would like to mention that I predicted the idea of foldable displays over 25 years ago in a computer training seminar by standing up, taking a piece of paper, winning over my lecturer, Mr. Kirsch, and telling him that in the near future, the displays will be as foldable as this piece of paper, which I then folded up and put in my pocket. Future foldable smartphones could offer thinner and more flexible displays, allowing users to unfold the device and take advantage of a larger display without sacrificing portability.

5G Connectivity: 5G networks are becoming more widespread and future smartphones are expected to come with 5G connectivity by default. Although it should be noted here that work is already being done on the development of a 6G network. This enables faster data transfer rates, lower latency, and better network stability, resulting in improved connectivity and smoother use of online services.

Artificial Intelligence (AI): AI is expected to play a bigger role in smartphone technology. Future smartphones may offer more advanced AI algorithms and features, such as improved voice recognition, personalized recommendations, intelligent power management, and advanced image processing capabilities.

Improved Camera Capabilities: Cameras are an important aspect of smartphones, and image quality and functionality are expected to continue to improve. Future smartphones may offer advanced camera lenses, sensors, and image processing technologies to enable better photos and videos in different lighting conditions, as well as advanced features such as optical zoom, night mode, and professional image editing.

Biometric authentication: Biometric authentication methods such as fingerprint sensors and face recognition are expected to continue to evolve and improve. Future smartphones may offer more advanced biometric sensors and algorithms to enable even more secure and convenient authentication.

Advanced Augmented Reality (AR): AR capabilities could play a bigger role in smartphones in the future. Future smartphones may offer enhanced AR capabilities, allowing users to seamlessly embed virtual objects into the real world and create interactive AR experiences.

But now we also need to address intentional obsolescence:

Intentional obsolescence of home appliances.

Intentional obsolescence refers to manufacturers' practice of deliberately designing products to have a finite lifespan and require faster replacement. There are different types of obsolescence, such as functional obsolescence (planned defects), stylistic obsolescence (fashion changes), and technical obsolescence (non-upgradable devices). Regarding the future of intentional obsolescence, there are a few trends and developments that are emerging:
Legal regulation: Measures to combat intentional obsolescence have already begun in some countries. Further legislation could be enacted to oblige manufacturers to extend product lifespans and to provide more transparent information about the lifespan of their products. I would even go as far as saying that every electrical device must have a life cycle sticker, just like the energy efficiency label. Then the customer would also have a transparent choice of choosing devices that last either 10 or 20 years.
Consumer Awareness: Consumer awareness of the issue of intentional obsolescence is increasing. More and more people are informed and are looking for more durable products or ways to repair or upgrade their

products. This could lead to an increasing demand for high-quality and durable products and force manufacturers to rethink.

Reparability and modular designs: Manufacturers could increasingly focus on repairable and modular product designs. By facilitating the repair and replacement of individual components, the lifespan of products can be extended. Some companies have already started adopting these approaches to meet consumer needs. Fortunately, the EU is already working on such a law.

Sharing economy and leasing models: The sharing economy and leasing models could help reduce the demand for short-lived products. When products are shared or leased, their lifespan can be extended as they are used by multiple users. This could lead to a shift in consumer behavior where the focus is on using products rather than owning them.

Technological Advances: Advances in technology could help create more durable and sustainable products. For example, materials that are more resilient or that can repair themselves could be used. Innovative recycling and resource management solutions could also help reduce the negative impact of intentional obsolescence.

At home:

Futuristic smart house.

Artificial intelligence will also find its way here.
Most electronic devices will be microprocessor controlled and integrated into a network, which can then be controlled via smartphone and voice commands.
Here are some more potential changes broken down in house technology in the future:
Intelligent home security and safety technology: The security technology for houses will continue to develop. Future technologies could include enhanced surveillance systems, smart alarm systems, biometric access control systems, facial recognition technologies, and artificial intelligence (AI) integration to detect suspicious behavior. The security against burglary will increase exorbitantly because the biometric signature of residents can be stored in the computer. So that when the resident leaves their home and "arms" the system, the house automatically turns off the stove and lights. In the event that a burglar tries to gain access to the property, the police will be informed and surveillance of the area will be activated via video. The number of

burglaries will drop very sharply. The same development will happen with cars, motorcycles and bicycles, all of which will be very easy to locate with a GPS tracking system.

Television: Television technology has evolved significantly over the years, and more changes are likely to occur in the future.
I am convinced that televisions with their fixed housings will also disappear completely. In the near future we will have true 3D hologram spatial representations. But until then, here are some possible developments:

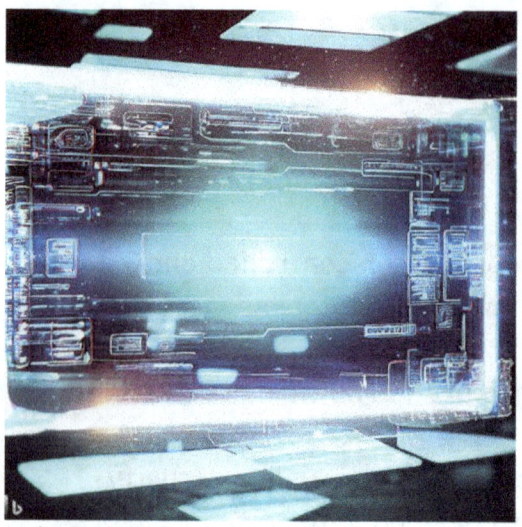
Holographic TV of the future.

Image Quality: Image quality will continue to improve. 4K and even 8K resolutions are already available today. In the future, even higher resolutions and advanced technologies such as OLED (Organic Light Emitting Diode) or Micro LED could be used to offer sharper, higher contrast and more vivid images.

Bigger screens: TVs could get even bigger as the technology to make big screens gets more advanced. TVs with screen sizes in excess of 100 inches are already available today and these sizes could continue to increase in the future.

Thin and Flexible Displays: TVs are expected to become thinner and more flexible in the future. Advances in display technology such as OLED allow TVs to be curved or even roll up. This would open up new possibilities for TV placement and design.
Incidentally, I was the one who won a curved LG OLED 4K in the annual competition 5 years ago. Splendid, isn't it?

Built-in smart technology: Smart TVs that are connected to the Internet and support various apps and streaming services are already widespread. In the future, televisions could be even more integrated into the smart home ecosystem. They could communicate with other smart devices in the home and be part of a networked home automation system, for example.

Interactivity and Virtual Reality: TVs could become more interactive and offer users a more immersive experience. Advances in virtual reality technology could allow viewers to immerse themselves in the television experience, such as playing interactive games or taking virtual trips.

Personalization and Recommendations: By using artificial intelligence and data analysis, TVs could offer personalized content and recommendations based on users' individual preferences and viewing habits. This could make it easier to discover new content and personalize the viewing experience.

Refrigerators: In the future, refrigerators are expected to see some technological advances and changes. Here are some possible technical developments:

Futuristic Smart Fridge.

Smart functions: Refrigerators will increasingly be equipped with smart functions. They can be connected to the internet to perform various tasks. For example, they could monitor grocery inventory, create grocery lists, suggest recipes, or send notifications when groceries run out or are approaching their sell-by dates. Imagine the refrigerator automatically writing milk or eggs on the shopping list and sending it to your smartphone. They could also communicate with other smart devices in the home to improve efficiency and usability.

Energy efficiency: Future refrigerators are expected to be even more energy efficient than today's models. Advances in insulation technology, compressors and refrigeration cycles can help reduce energy consumption. In addition, sensors and algorithms could be used to adapt the operation of the refrigerator to usage habits and to avoid unnecessary energy consumption.

Sustainability: With a growing awareness of environmental issues, future refrigerators are likely to use more sustainable materials and manufacturing processes. Recycling and reuse options could be implemented for certain components. In addition, refrigerators could offer opportunities to reduce food waste, for example through better storage or intelligent use-by-date monitoring.

Design and flexibility: Future refrigerators could also change in terms of their design and flexibility. Modular concepts could be introduced in which individual components, such as e.g. B. additional fridge or freezer drawers can be added or removed as needed. This enables adaptation to individual requirements and prevents overcapacity or lack of space. For example, it would be possible to assemble a refrigerator from modules, 4 modules refrigerator and 1 module freezer.

Improved storage and freshness: Advances in refrigeration technology could mean food can be kept fresher for longer. For example, innovative cooling systems, air circulation or special compartments for certain food categories could improve the shelf life and quality of the food.
The future has already arrived in building and construction technology and further progress and changes are expected to take place.

Sustainability and energy efficiency: With the increasing need to address climate change, sustainability and energy efficiency in building technology will play a key role. Buildings could be made more energy efficient, with improved insulation materials, energy efficient lighting, renewable energy sources such as solar power, and intelligent energy management systems that optimize energy use.

Smart buildings and automation: Advances in automation technology and the Internet of Things (IoT) could lead to smarter buildings.

Buildings could be equipped with sensors, data analytics and automated systems to optimize energy use, adjust indoor climate and improve occupant comfort. For example, intelligent lighting systems, heating and air conditioning systems or automatic window controls could be implemented.

Modular building and 3D printing: Modular building and the use of 3D printing technology could increase in the future. Modular buildings allow for faster and more efficient construction processes as the modules can be pre-produced in factories and then assembled on site. 3D printing can make it easier to build complex structures and reduce material waste.

Smart urban design: In the context of urban growth, urban planners and architects could integrate intelligent technologies into the design of neighborhoods and building complexes. Smart cities could offer better infrastructure for transport, energy supply, waste disposal and resource management. The aim would be to improve the quality of life, use resources more efficiently and promote sustainability.

Innovative Building Materials: New building materials could be developed to revolutionize construction technology. For example, stronger, lighter, and more flexible materials could be used. Innovative design could also encourage the use of sustainable and recycled materials.

Resilience and adaptability: In the face of increasing challenges posed by climate change, buildings could be designed to be more resilient and adaptable. This may include improved structures to withstand natural disasters, as well as strategies to adapt to changing climatic conditions such as heat or heavy rain.

Landscape architecture:

Sustainable, environmentally conscious landscape architecture.

Landscape architecture is constantly changing, which is influenced by various factors. Here are some possible changes that could occur in the future:

Sustainability and environmental awareness: Future landscape architecture is expected to be more focused on sustainability and environmental awareness. There will be an increased use of natural resources, green infrastructure and resource-saving technologies. The focus will be on creating vibrant, ecologically valuable and resilient landscapes.

Climate Change Adaptation: With the increasing impacts of climate change, landscape architects will increasingly take action to adapt to changing climatic conditions. This may include creating green spaces to cool urban spaces, integrating storm water management into design, and protecting against coastal flooding.

Technological Innovations: The use of new technologies will influence landscape architecture in many ways. For example, computer-aided design and simulation tools can be used to analyze and plan complex ecosystems. The use of drones to take pictures of the terrain or intelligent systems for irrigation and maintenance of landscapes are also conceivable.

Urban Farming and Vertical Gardens: Given the increasing demand for food and the limited availability of cultivable land, landscape architects could increasingly focus on urban farming and vertical gardens. By integrating agricultural land into urban spaces, food can be produced locally and the carbon footprint reduced.

Vertical garden of the future.

Natural design and biodiversity: Promoting biodiversity and integrating natural elements into design will continue to play an important role in the future. Landscape architects could pay more attention to native plant species and the creation of habitats for animal and plant species in order to preserve and promote biological diversity.

These changes are just a few examples of how landscape architecture might evolve in the future.

.... **but now to a sensitive topic, and please don't be alarmed.**

Cooking:
Further advances and changes in cooking technology are expected to take place in the future. Here are some possible developments:

Automation: Cooking technology could be increasingly automated. Advances in robotics and artificial intelligence could lead to smart kitchen appliances that can do certain tasks automatically. For example, robots could do the cutting, stirring and mixing of ingredients while the chef focuses on creative aspects.

All in one automatic cooker.

Smart kitchen appliances: Kitchen appliances could be increasingly integrated into the Internet of Things (IoT). Smart kitchen appliances could be connected to an app or voice control and allow users to control appliances remotely, retrieve recipes or monitor the cooking process.

Automatic kitchen of the future.

Precision Cooking: Precision cooking, where temperatures and cooking times are precisely controlled, could be further developed in the future. Sous-vide cookers, which are currently popular, could be further improved, and new technologies could make it possible to achieve more precise and even heat transfer.

Sustainability and environmental awareness: In view of growing environmental problems, sustainability in cooking technology will play a greater role. Energy-efficient kitchen appliances could be developed that reduce energy consumption. Alternative and sustainable cooking methods could also be increasingly used, such as solar cooking devices or cooking with renewable energies.

Personalized Nutrition: With advances in genetics and personalized medicine, cooking technology could also be geared toward personalized nutrition. Technologies could be developed to take people's individual dietary needs and preferences into account and automatically suggest tailored recipes or meals.

Virtual Reality and Augmented Reality: Virtual reality and augmented reality could be used in cooking technology to enable virtual cooking classes, interactive tutorials and immersive cooking experiences. With the help of VR glasses, people could virtually immerse themselves in different kitchens or cooking environments and be guided by experts.

Futuristic cooking: I would even dare and predict that in the distant future our food will come out of a 3D printer on our plates. You choose a recipe from the internet or an internal database, and after a few minutes the dish comes out of the 3D printer as shown in the picture.

Smart home integration: The integration of smart home technologies will continue to increase. This includes connecting devices, sensors and systems in the home to enable seamless control and automation. Examples of smart home technologies include intelligent lighting systems, heating and air conditioning controls, smart home security systems, connected home appliances, and voice control systems.

3D food printers will be popular.

Energy efficiency and sustainability: The use of energy-efficient and sustainable technologies will play a greater role. This includes the use of solar panels to generate electricity, energy-efficient heating and cooling systems, intelligent energy management systems to monitor and optimize energy consumption, energy storage solutions, rainwater treatment systems and the integration of smart grid technologies.

Health and Wellness Technologies: The integration of technologies to improve health and well-being in homes will become more important. This can include the integration of health monitoring systems, indoor air quality measurements, lighting systems to support the sleep cycle, smart fitness devices and smart kitchen appliances to promote healthy eating.

Future wellness oasis.

Voice control and artificial intelligence: The integration of voice control systems such as Amazon Alexa, Google Assistant or Apple Siri is becoming increasingly popular. Future technologies could offer improved speech recognition and seamless integration of artificial intelligence (AI) to enable intelligent assistance functions, personalized recommendations and automated processes in the home.

Virtual Reality (VR) and Augmented Reality (AR): VR and AR technologies could be increasingly used in homes in the future. This could provide the ability to experience virtual environments, augment home theater systems, conduct property tours in virtual reality, or use AR elements for home improvement projects and interior design. After our home, what is the second most important thing?

Advanced VR technology.

Our Jobs:
But what will our jobs look like in the future?

The workplace is expected to experience some significant changes in the future, influenced by technological advances, automation, shifting demographics and changing work models. Here are some possible developments:

Automation and Artificial Intelligence (AI): Advances in automation and AI could lead to increased use of machines and robots to take over repetitive and routine tasks. This may result in some traditional jobs being replaced by machines. At the same time, however, new job opportunities can arise as the cooperation between humans and machines creates new areas of responsibility.

Factory with 3D printer.

New skills and qualifications: As the world of work changes, new skills and qualifications will also be required. Soft skills such as creativity, problem-solving skills, emotional intelligence and intercultural skills are becoming increasingly important as they are traits that are difficult for machines to emulate. Technological skills and the ability to use digital tools are also becoming increasingly important.

Flexible working and digitization: Digitization enables people to work more flexibly and to be independent of a fixed location. Remote work, freelancing and the gig economy could continue to gain traction. This opens up opportunities for more flexibility and work-life balance, but also requires new approaches to managing teams and maintaining collaboration.

Lifelong learning: In view of the rapid changes in the world of work, lifelong learning is becoming increasingly important. People will need to continually up skill and acquire new skills to keep up with the demands of the changing workplace. Continuing education programs, online courses and other forms of learning are expected to gain in importance.

New workspaces and industries: Technological advances can also foster the creation of new workspaces and industries. For example, areas such as renewable energy, artificial intelligence, robotics, data analytics, cyber security and virtual reality could offer new job opportunities. At the same time, traditional industries may restructure or disappear while others grow.

It is important to understand that the changes depend on various factors such as technological developments, political decisions, economic conditions and societal changes. It is possible that some jobs may will be lost while others are created or transformed. Flexibility, adaptability and lifelong learning will be important factors to be successful in the changing world of work.

So next we need to take a look at the tools.

Tools: In the future, tools are expected to undergo some technological advances and changes. Here are some possible developments:

Automation and robotics: tools could be increasingly automated and robotic. This means they are able to perform certain tasks autonomously or be assisted by robots. Automated tools can improve efficiency and accuracy and reduce human workload.

Artificial Intelligence (AI): Tools could be equipped with AI capabilities to better analyze, plan and perform specific tasks. For example, AI-controlled tools can use pattern recognition to avoid errors or to find optimal solutions to complex problems.

3D printing and additive manufacturing: The use of 3D printing and additive manufacturing technology could transform the way tools are made. These technologies allow tools to be made quickly and individually, rather than relying on mass production and warehousing. This can lead to customized solutions and a faster development process.

Soon at home everywhere.

Integrated sensors and IoT connectivity: Future tools could be equipped with integrated sensors that provide information about the state of the tool, the working environment or the progress of a task. This data could be collected and analyzed over the Internet of Things (IoT) to improve the performance and security of the tools.

Augmented Reality (AR) and Virtual Reality (VR): AR and VR technologies could be integrated into tools to provide users with additional information and assistance in performing tasks. For example, AR glasses could display instructions, virtual blueprints, or visual cues to improve accuracy and efficiency.

Sustainability: In an increasingly environmentally conscious world, tools are likely to be designed to be more sustainable. This could include using greener materials, improving energy efficiency, and developing tools that are more durable and repairable.

These changes are possible scenarios of how tools might evolve in the future. The exact advances and innovations of various factors depend on technological breakthroughs, market demands, economic conditions and legal regulations. However, the tool industry will continue to evolve to meet the demands of the changing world of work.

Shopping will also change:

In the future, supermarkets and shopping malls are expected to undergo some changes. Here are some possible developments:

Technology and Automation: Advances in technology, especially in the field of robotics and artificial intelligence, could lead to increased automation in supermarkets and shopping malls. This could include, for example, the use of self-driving shopping carts, automated checkout systems or robots for shelf filling and warehouse management.

Personalization and data analysis: By using customer loyalty programs, mobile apps and data analysis, supermarkets and shopping centers can offer personalized shopping experiences. Customers could receive specific recommendations based on their preferences and shopping habits.

Online Shopping and Delivery: The trend towards online shopping is expected to increase further. Supermarkets and malls could increase their presence in e-commerce and offer more delivery services to offer more convenience to customers.

Sustainability: Because of increasing environmental problems, sustainability will be an important factor for supermarkets and shopping centers. They are expected to take steps to reduce their environmental impact, such as using energy-efficient lighting systems, increasing the use of renewable energy and reducing packaging waste.

Experience-oriented shopping: To attract customers, supermarkets and shopping centers could increasingly rely on experience-oriented shopping. This could include the creation of cozy shopping areas, restaurants, entertainment venues, events, or interactive technologies to provide a fun shopping experience.

Clothing is a big part of shopping:

The textile processing and fashion industries are expected to experience some significant changes in the future. Here are some possible developments:

Sustainable materials and production processes: Given the growing environmental awareness, the use of sustainable materials and production processes in the textile processing and fashion industry is becoming increasingly important. There could be an increased use of recycled materials, organic and biodegradable fabrics, as well as innovative materials such as fabrics made from marine debris or mushroom leather. The introduction of eco-friendly dyeing methods and energy-efficient manufacturing processes can also play a role.

Technological Innovations: Technological advances can change the way clothes are made, designed, and worn. For example, 3D printing and digital cutting patterns can make production processes more efficient and tailored. Smart fabrics and textiles can offer functions such as temperature control, moisture management, or sensor-based properties. Wearable technology, such as clothing with integrated electronics or sensors, could also become more important.

On-Demand Production and Customization: With the advent of technologies such as 3D printing and digital fabrication, customized and tailored garments could become more accessible. Customers could personalize their clothing online and have it made directly to order. This could lead to a reduction in overproduction, waste and inventory.

Sharing economy and rental models: The sharing economy is already having an impact on various industries, including fashion. Clothing rental and loaner models could continue to grow in the future. Customers could rent garments for some time instead of buying them, which can reduce resource consumption and environmental impact.

E-Commerce and Virtual Trying On: The trend towards online shopping is expected to continue, bringing about a change in the way clothes are selected and bought. Virtual try-on opportunities, where customers can provide their avatars with their body measurements, could help them better assess the fit and appearance of clothing.

Fashion as a Service: Instead of owning clothes, customers could use subscription services where they have access to a rotating selection of clothing items. This can reduce the pressure to constantly repurchase clothes and shift the focus to the usefulness and useful life of clothes.

Also worth mentioning is our music and the accompanying sound technology:

Audio technology is constantly evolving, and some interesting changes can be expected in the future. Here are some possible developments:

Immersive Sound Experiences: As technology advances, immersive sound experiences could become more important. Advances in 3D audio technology, virtual reality (VR) and augmented reality (AR) could mean that we can experience music and sound effects even more immersive. This could open up new possibilities for the creation and playback of music and the design of sound experiences.

Headphones with built-in AI.

Artificial Intelligence (AI) and Machine Learning: AI and machine learning could play a bigger role in audio engineering. For example, AI algorithms could help with sound optimization, noise reduction, mixing, and mastering. Automated processes and AI-driven tools could improve the workflow for audio engineers and music producers and save time.

Higher Resolution and Audio Quality: With the advancement of audio technology, we might experience higher resolution and audio quality in the future. This includes improved clarity, precision, and dynamics in the sound. Advances in audio codecs and audio compression techniques could result in better sound reproduction, whether on streaming services, in hi-fi systems or in live performances.

Wireless transmission and network integration: Wireless transmission of audio content is becoming increasingly popular and this trend is expected to continue. Future audio technology could use wireless connections to transmit audio signals without the limitations of cables. In addition, network integration and wireless control capabilities could improve the flexibility and connectivity of audio systems.

Personalized Sound Experience: As technology advances, we may be able to customize the way we sound. Advances in sound processing and personalized audio technologies could make it possible to tailor sound to our individual listening habits, preferences, and physiological characteristics.

Sustainable audio technology: Given the growing environmental awareness, sustainability in audio technology could also play a greater role. Greener production processes, materials and energy-saving technologies could be developed to reduce resource consumption and environmental impact.

The exact changes in audio engineering depend on technological breakthroughs, market needs and creative innovations. The future of audio engineering will likely be shaped by a combination of these and other developments.

Print Media:
While I don't think books will disappear completely, printing technology, books and magazines have already undergone significant changes in recent years and this trend will likely continue in the future. Here are some possible developments:

Digital Transformation: With the advent of digital technologies, many publications have already shifted to digital formats. In the future, this trend could increase further, leading to lower demand for printed books and magazines. E-books, e-magazines, and other electronic publications could become more important.

On-demand printing: On-demand printing technology makes it possible to print books and magazines in shorter runs or even individually as needed. This could result in a reduction in printing costs, less warehousing, and greater publishing flexibility.

Books of the future with animations.

Personalized and interactive content: With advances in printing technology, personalized and interactive elements could become more integrated into books and magazines. For example, books could be equipped with augmented reality (AR) or virtual reality (VR) functions to enable an interactive reading experience. Personalized books, tailored to individual preferences and interests, could also become more important.

Sustainability and eco-friendly materials: With growing environmental awareness, printing technology could become more sustainable in the future. The use of environmentally friendly printing methods, recyclable materials, and ecologically responsible inks could become more important to reduce the environmental impact.

Hybrid Formats: Future releases could combine different media and formats. For example, books and magazines could contain complementary online content, videos, or multimedia elements. This could lead to greater integration of digital and printed media.

Niche publications and collectibles: In a digital world, printed books and magazines could acquire special value as collectibles or as high-quality, exclusive publications. Niche publications with limited circulation and specialized topics could continue to play a role.

The future of print technology is likely to be shaped by a mix of digital and print media, with readers' needs and preferences playing an important role.
However, with shopping comes a great deal of responsibility. I mean environmental protection with all sub-topics such as microplastics in the oceans, waste avoidance and recycling.
Cleaning the oceans and removing microplastics are major challenges that are being addressed around the world. In the future, different

approaches and technologies could be used to combat these problems. Here are some possible developments:

Improved monitoring and detection: Advances in technology could lead to improved monitoring of marine pollution and the spread of microplastics. Satellites, drones and sensors could be deployed to gather precise data on pollution and identify hotspots. This could help in the planning and implementation of cleaning measures.

More efficient cleaning technologies: More efficient and scalable technologies for cleaning the oceans and removing microplastics could be developed in the future. This includes for example, improved waste collection systems that are specially designed to capture microplastic particles. These technologies could work autonomously and effectively clean large areas.

Biodegradation Technologies: The development of biodegradation technologies could help ensure that microplastics are naturally degraded in the sea. Research is focused on enzymes and microorganisms capable of breaking down plastics. These approaches could be used in the future to break down and remove microplastics in water.

Filtering and wastewater treatment: Improved wastewater treatment systems could be used to reduce the amount of micro plastics entering the oceans. Advanced filtration technologies could be integrated into wastewater treatment plants to remove microplastics from wastewater before it reaches the sea.

Education and awareness-raising: A long-term solution to cleaning up the oceans and reducing microplastics also requires a change in human behavior. Increased education and awareness-raising about the impact of plastic pollution and the importance of protecting the environment could help people use plastic more responsibly and reduce the consumption of single-use products.

Cooperation and international initiatives: Tackling ocean pollution requires global cooperation. International initiatives, government programs, and partnerships between governments, companies and non-governmental organizations could be strengthened in the future to develop common solutions and pool resources for cleaning the oceans and removing micro plastics.
It should be noted here that combating ocean pollution effectively does not depend on a few countries, but success depends on all countries without exception.

Film and entertainment industries:

Film production and the entertainment industry are in constant flux, and we can expect some exciting changes in the future. Here are some possible developments:

Streaming and on-demand content: The trend towards streaming and on-demand content is expected to continue to grow. Platforms like Netflix, Amazon Prime Video, Disney+ and others have already changed viewer behavior. Going forward, traditional cinemas could continue to lose importance while streaming services produce and release even more original content.

Virtual Reality (VR) and Augmented Reality (AR): VR and AR could play a bigger role in film production and entertainment. Movies and TV series could offer immersive VR experiences where viewers can dive right into the action. AR could also play a role in advertising, live events and interaction with virtual characters.

Personalized Content and Interactive Experiences: As technology advances, personalized content and interactive experiences could increase in the entertainment space. For example, viewers could make choices that affect the course of a story, or receive personalized ads and recommendations based on their individual preferences.

Artificial intelligence (AI) and machine learning: AI and machine learning could revolutionize film production and entertainment. AI algorithms could be used in film analysis and prediction, film editing, visual effects generation, and music composition. The use of digital avatars or AI-controlled actors is also conceivable.

Advances in Visual Effects and CGI: Technological advances in visual effects (VFX) and computer generated imagery (CGI) could allow for even more realistic and immersive movie experiences in the future. Virtual sets could replace real sets, and digital actors could become almost indistinguishable from real actors.

International collaboration and global content:
With increasing globalization and digital networking, collaboration between filmmakers and producers from different countries and cultures could be intensified. This could lead to a greater variety of international content and easier access to films and series from all over the world.

Sustainability and Green Practices: As environmental awareness grows, the film production and entertainment industries may have a greater focus on sustainability. Measures such as the use of renewable energy on the film set, environmentally friendly production processes and the reduction of plastic waste could become more important.

So what's going to happen to all that junk?
The previous Recycling system has demonstrably failed.
Waste prevention and recycling are important aspects of waste management that can be further developed in the future. Here are some changes and trends that are needed:

Circular economy: An increasing spread of the concept of the circular economy is to be expected. Instead of treating waste as trash, it tries to keep materials and resources in closed loops. Products should be designed in such a way that they can be reused, recycled or, biodegraded instead of being disposed of at the end of their lifespan.

Packaging Reduction: Packaging waste represents a significant proportion of waste generation. In the future, there could be an increased focus on reducing packaging materials and promoting more environmentally friendly alternatives such as biodegradable or compostable packaging. In addition, innovative technologies such as 3D printing could help create bespoke packaging and reduce the need for excess packaging.

Advanced Recycling: As technology advances, new processes and methods could be developed to increase recycling efficiency. Advanced sorting and separation technologies could make it possible to recycle a wider range of materials and achieve a higher quality of recycled material. Chemical recycling, in which plastics are broken down into their chemical components for reuse, could also become more important.

Digital Technologies: The use of digital technologies such as the Internet of Things (IoT) and blockchain could enable better traceability and monitoring of waste streams. This could help manage waste more efficiently, fight illegal disposal and make the whole recycling process more transparent.

Awareness and Education: Increased awareness and education about the importance of waste prevention and recycling could help increase people's awareness and engagement. Campaigns to raise awareness of recycling practices and promote sustainable consumption could be further expanded in the future to achieve broader participation.

Regulatory Action: Governments need to take more regulatory action to encourage waste prevention and recycling. This could include the introduction of stricter packaging disposal regulations, the introduction of waste sorting schemes, or financial incentives for companies that adopt sustainable practices.

Renewable Raw Materials:

As a logical conclusion we should pay attention to guiding renewable raw materials.

Technological Advances: Advances in agricultural practices, biotechnology, and genetic modification can lead to increased efficiency and productivity in the extraction of renewable resources. For example, improved cultivation techniques, plant varieties, or biotechnological processes could increase crop yields.

Sustainability and environmental aspects: Given the increasing environmental problems and climate change, it is expected that the focus on sustainable cultivation methods and environmentally friendly production processes will increase. This could reduce the use of pesticides and fertilizers, optimize water use and promote biodiversity protection.

New areas of application: In the future, renewable raw materials could be increasingly used in new sectors and areas of application. For example, they could increasingly serve as raw materials for the production of bioplastics, bio-based chemicals, renewable energies or pharmaceutical products. This would lead to a greater variety of products based on renewable raw materials.

International trade and political framework: The demand for renewable raw materials can be influenced by international trade and the political framework. Trade agreements, tariffs, or subsidies can change the market for renewable raw materials and influence production in different countries.

Change in consumer behavior: An increasing demand for sustainable products could lead to increased use of renewable raw materials. If consumers prefer greener options and companies respond, it could lead to greater demand for renewable resources.

Hospitals and nursing:
There will also be significant changes in the field of nursing. A computer then will monitor the vital signs and medication of old people or people in need of care and, if necessary, an emergency alarm is automatically triggered.
In surgery, too, there will be rapid development in the field of computer-assisted surgery and nanotechnology. Let's also consider that computers will eventually be able to remove cell-specific tumors, which would not be possible with human motor skills. Or in the field of Nano computer technology, where there will then be miniaturized robots that can independently recognize clogged arteries and free them from e.g. fat deposits.
The sensors and mechanics of prostheses are being revolutionized by further development.

Bionics:
The use of bionics in the medical field has already made significant progress in recent years and is expected to continue to grow in the future. Bionics, also known as biomimetics, refers to the application of biological principles and structures to engineered systems to create innovative solutions. In the medical field, this can include the development of bionic prostheses, implants, tissue regeneration techniques, and diagnostic tools.

Here are some possible developments we might see related to the use of bionics in the medical field in the future:

Bionic Prostheses: Advances in bionics could lead to increasingly advanced and functional bionic prostheses. By integrating sensors and actuators, prostheses can allow for more natural movements and sensations.

Neuroprostheses: Bionics may also play a role in the development of neuroprostheses that allow people with SCI or other neurological impairments to regain movement or function. This could include connecting prostheses directly to the nervous system or the brain.

Organ and tissue regeneration: Bionics can help to develop new techniques for regenerating organs and tissue. This could include the use of biomimetic materials, stem cell therapy, or 3D bioprinting to replace or repair damaged or diseased tissues.

Hearing Restoration: I think deaf people will be able to hear again because there will be Nano transmitters and receivers that convert the sound signal from an external transmitter directly into an impulse and then implement the information in the appropriate area of the brain. The same will also make it possible for the blind to see again.

Vision Restoration: It uses artificial eyes consisting of a high-resolution camera and transmitter, and the signals are then transmitted directly to the brain's visual center.

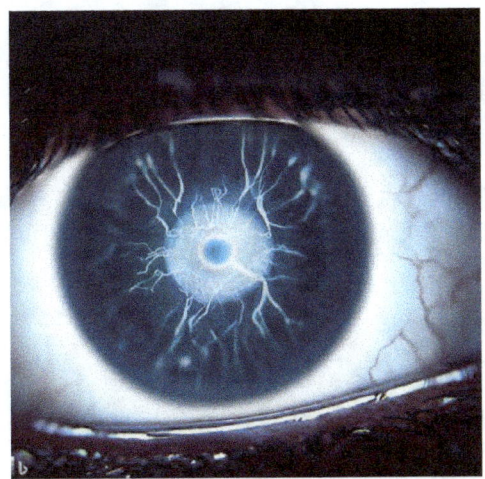
Contact lens that projects the image onto the retina.

Diagnostics and imaging: Bionics can also play a role in the development of advanced diagnostic tools and imaging techniques. By applying biological principles, more precise, non-invasive diagnostic methods can be developed that enable early disease detection and individualized treatment approaches.

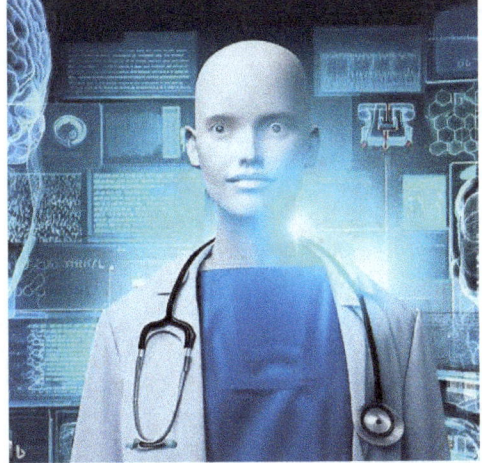
AI is also finding its way into diagnostics.

Diagnostics: AI will also find its way into diagnostics. Imagine that in the future there will be hospitals where artificial intelligence will take over the diagnosis. The diagnosis will be like walking into a room and then being scanned by computers for any symptoms or abnormalities, viruses, bacteria, and pathogens.

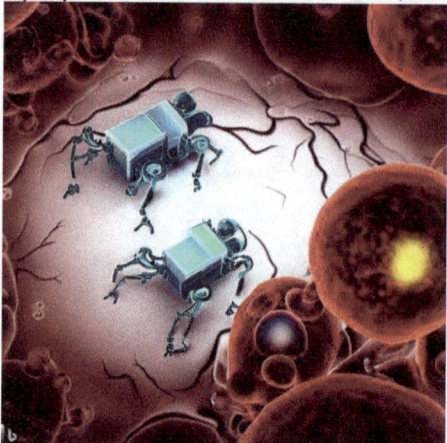
Nano and micro robots in action.

Robotics in surgery: Bionics can support the development of robotic systems used in surgery. Robot-assisted surgery enables more precise interventions and can improve the accuracy and safety of medical procedures.

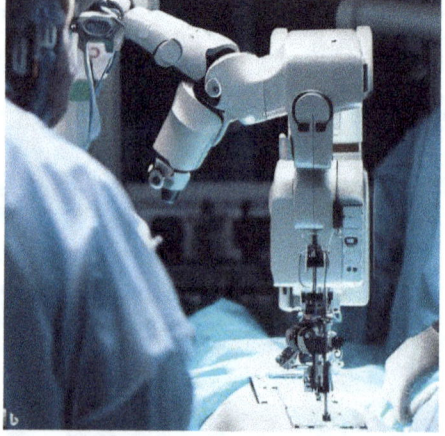
Computer assisted surgeries are becoming a lot performed more precisely than by human hands.

Now to the very sensitive topic of life expectancy.

The issue of life expectancy is very controversial because it involves so many aspects and is influenced by a variety of factors, including medical advances, socioeconomic conditions, lifestyle, environmental factors and access to healthcare. It is important to note that the future development of life expectancy is uncertain and depends on many variable factors. Nevertheless, there are some trends and possible changes that can be discussed:

Medical Advances: Advances in medicine, particularly in the areas of prevention, diagnosis, and treatment of disease, could increase life expectancy in the future. The development of new therapies, medicines and technologies, could help fight diseases better and improve the quality of life in old age.

Improved healthcare: Access to quality healthcare can have a significant impact on life expectancy. Improved health infrastructure, better availability of health services, and better care for diseases could help increase life expectancy.

Lifestyle and prevention: A healthy lifestyle and preventive measures play an important role in life expectancy. A balanced diet, regular physical activity, not smoking and excessive alcohol consumption, and protection from pollution can reduce the risk of diseases and contribute to a longer lifespan.

Socioeconomic factors: Socioeconomic conditions, such as education, income, and social support, can affect life expectancy. Higher levels of education and better socio-economic conditions are often associated with longer life expectancies as they allow better access to resources and health care.

Demographic changes: Demographic changes, such as the aging of the population, can affect life expectancy. As societies age, there may be increased demand for age-appropriate health services and social support, which may have a positive impact on life expectancy.

Not to forget that there can be regional and population-related differences and that there are limits to how much life expectancy can increase. Various factors such as genetic predisposition, environmental factors and random events also play a role. The exact future of life expectancy, therefore, remains uncertain and can be influenced by a variety of factors.

The development and implementation of bionic technologies in the medical field must also be accompanied by ethical, legal, and social considerations. Privacy, security, accessibility, and the integration of these technologies into the healthcare system are important aspects that need to be considered.

Even if it sounds very futuristic now, I am firmly convinced that such systems will exist in the near future.

The Transport Systems:

Further development of car technology: As some car companies are already showing us, in the near future all the cars we know will only exist in museums.
Cars will all be electric in the future. The battery system in the car will not prevail either. I think there will be an induction system in streets that will generate electricity directly in the vehicle, which has the advantage that we no longer need heavy batteries and the weight of a car is reduced to a few hundred kilograms. The onboard computer will also determine whether the driver is drunk and no longer able to drive and then, if necessary, steer the vehicle home autonomously so that there will be no more traffic accidents due to truck driving. There will also be many changes in commercial road haulage.

Futuristic car.   Futuristic cockpit.

Motorcycles: Further advances and changes in motorcycle technology are expected to take place in the future.

Electrification: With the increased focus on sustainability and environmental protection, the electrification of motorcycles is expected to progress. Electric motorcycles are already gaining popularity, and in the future technological advances could lead to the improved range, performance and charging infrastructure.

Connectivity and integration of technology: Motorcycles could be more equipped with technology and connectivity. For example, they could be connected to the Internet and offer features such as navigation, music streaming, smartphone integration, and wireless communication. Intelligent assistance systems and safety technologies such as adaptive cruise control or lane departure warning systems could also find their way into motorcycles.

Lightweight construction and material innovations: Advances in material technology could lead to lighter yet more durable motorcycles. The use of composites, carbon fiber or other innovative materials could reduce weight and improve performance.

Autonomous driving: While autonomous driving on motorized two-wheelers represents a particular challenge, assisted driving systems could be developed in the future that offers the driver more safety and support. These systems could, for example, help stabilize the motorcycle in critical situations or take over driving in certain traffic scenarios.

Safety Technologies: Advances in sensor technology and image processing could lead to improved safety on motorcycles. Collision warning systems, adaptive lighting, smart brakes, and lane detection systems could be developed to reduce accidents and improve driver safety.

Customization and adaptability: In the future, motorcycles could be even more customizable. The ability to customize design, seating position, riding modes and chassis settings could allow riders to tailor their motorcycle to their personal preferences and riding needs.

Road haulage: I think the most dangerous factor, is that human will no longer drive trucks. The truck driver as such will no longer exist. Rather, there will be autonomous transporters or trucks that are guided to their destination with pinpoint accuracy by computers with AI and GPS.

Road freight transport, especially road freight transport, is expected to experience various changes and advances in the future to improve efficiency, sustainability and safety. Here are some possible developments we might see in the future:

Electrification and alternative drives: Electric drive systems are expected to play a greater role in road haulage. Electric trucks and delivery vehicles are increasingly being used to reduce the use of fossil fuels and reduce emissions. In addition, alternative drives such as hydrogen or fuel cells could be used to offer a zero-emission or low-emission transport solution.

Autonomous road haulage of the future.

Automation and autonomous vehicles: Automation will also increase road haulage. Advances in artificial intelligence and sensor technology enable the use of autonomous trucks and delivery vehicles. These vehicles can operate without human drivers, allowing for more efficient and safer logistics.

Connectivity and telematics: The integration of connectivity and telematics will continue to play an important role. Through the use of wireless communication technology, vehicles can be monitored in real-time. This enables optimized route planning, improved traffic control and more efficient vehicle fleet management.

Efficient Route Management: Future technologies could include advanced route management systems that take traffic congestion, road conditions, and weather forecasts into account to determine the most efficient routes for freight transport. This can help reduce delays and save fuel.

Electronic freight documents and digital tracking: The digitization of freight documents and the introduction of digital tracking systems can improve the entire logistics process. Electronic freight documents and digital platforms enable efficient tracking of freight, better transparency and faster handling of transport operations.

Sustainable logistics: Sustainability will play an increasingly important role in road haulage. Companies will strive to make their transport activities more environmentally friendly. This can be achieved through the use of renewable energy in logistics centers, the use of more environmentally friendly packaging, the optimization of routes, and the use of environmentally friendly vehicles and propulsion systems.

These developments aim to make road haulage more efficient, safer, and more environmentally friendly, thereby reducing costs and improving the environmental impact.

Aviation:
Aircraft technology is expected to undergo significant changes and advances in the future to improve aircraft efficiency, safety, sustainability, and comfort. Here are some possible developments we might see in the future:
There will be no more air traffic in the local area since the rail system will also change. There will be fast maglev trains and trains that will take you from Hamburg to Munich in just 90 minutes.
In aviation there will also be many changes shortly. I am thinking, for example, of the drive technology. Through the use of artificial intelligence, highly efficient electric motors are being developed that will replace the use of fossil fuels. Which of course will also greatly reduce exhaust emissions and noise pollution.

Airplane with electric or ion propulsion.

Electrification and Alternative Propulsion: Electric propulsion systems are expected to play a larger role in aviation. Hybrid and all-electric aircraft could replace traditional internal combustion engines, resulting in reduced emissions and noise. The use of hydrogen as a fuel for aircraft is also being explored as it is potentially emission-free.

Lightweight construction and new materials: The use of lighter materials such as carbon fiber composites, aluminum alloys, and advanced plastics will increase. This allows aircraft to become lighter, which reduces fuel consumption and improves efficiency. New materials can also improve resistance to fatigue and corrosion.

Aerodynamics and Aircraft Design: Advances in aerodynamics and aircraft design will help reduce drag and improve efficiency. New wing configurations, improved flow guidance, and innovative design approaches can reduce drag and lower fuel consumption.

Automation and autonomous aircraft: Automation will continue to play an important role. Advances in artificial intelligence and avionics are enabling the development of autonomous aircraft capable of autonomous takeoff, landing, and flight maneuvers. This could improve safety, increase air traffic capacity and assist the pilot in complex tasks.

Passenger comfort and interior design: Passenger comfort will have a high priority. Future airplanes could feature more advanced cabins that offer more legroom, better seats, improved entertainment systems, wireless internet, and larger windows. New technologies such as virtual reality (VR) and augmented reality (AR) can further improve the flight experience.

Sustainability and environmental friendliness: The aviation industry will strive to reduce its environmental impact. This includes the reduction of greenhouse gas emissions, noise reduction, and the use of more sustainable operating practices. Improved engines, more efficient flight routes, greener airport infrastructure, and the use of biofuels are some of the measures that can be taken.

Shipping and sea Cargo:
In the future, shipping technology is expected to undergo significant changes to improve ship efficiency, safety and sustainability. Here are some possible developments we might see in the future:

Alternative fuels: With efforts to reduce greenhouse gas emissions, shipping will increasingly use alternative fuels. These include, for example, liquefied natural gas (LNG), hydrogen, ammonia and electric propulsion systems. The transition to cleaner fuel options will help significantly reduce the environmental impact of shipping.

Electrification and hybrid propulsion: Electric propulsion systems and hybrid technologies will gain importance in shipping. By using electric motors in combination with batteries or fuel cells, ships can be operated with zero or fewer emissions. This helps reduce CO_2 emissions and improve air quality.

Automation and autonomous ships: The automation of ships will continue to advance. Advances in artificial intelligence (AI) and robotics are enabling the deployment of autonomous ships that can operate without a human crew. These ships use advanced sensors, data processing systems, and autonomous decision-making to safely navigate and transport cargo.

Increasing efficiency through digitization: Digitization will play a key role in improving efficiency in shipping. By integrating sensors, data analysis, and real-time communication, ship operations can be optimized and fuel consumption, maintenance costs, and environmental impact reduced. Big Data, the Internet of Things (IoT), and AI are used to collect and analyze data from various sources to make informed decisions and maximize performance.

Increased use of environmentally friendly materials and technologies:
The shipbuilding industry will increasingly rely on environmentally friendly materials and technologies. Lighter materials such as composites can reduce the weight of ships and reduce fuel consumption. New coatings can reduce resistance in the water and reduce energy consumption. In addition, environmentally friendly waste treatment and recycling technologies are used to minimize the environmental impact.

Improved safety systems and navigation technologies: Safety at sea will continue to be a priority. Advances in sensor, communications and navigation technology allow for better monitoring of ship traffic and avoidance of collisions.

Another point I would like to mention here is that in the near future, all motor vehicles such as cars, trucks, and motorcycles will be equipped with dash cams. It is incomprehensible to me why no insurance company has yet approached the legislature and made an application in this direction. Especially since it would save the insurance companies and consequently the amount payer a lot of money.

Environmental Technologies:
In the coming decades, computer technology and artificial intelligence will increasingly influence environmental protection and the development of materials that are 100% biodegradable thanks to Nanotechnology.

Nowadays, many products are far too harmful to the environment to be used much longer. Here are just a few examples soda cans that waste a lot of energy in manufacturing, and all those plastic bottles and containers for any product. AI will also play a major role in the development of new climate-neutral packaging. Just think of the many possibilities in Nanomaterial research and the development of completely new properties.

Soon, packaging technologies will continue to evolve to meet growing demands for sustainability, efficiency, and consumer safety. Here are some possible developments we might see in this area:

Sustainable Packaging Materials: With increasing concerns about pollution and resource consumption, the development of sustainable packaging materials will be a priority. This can include the use of bio-based plastics, compostable or biodegradable materials, recyclable packaging and reusable systems.

Smart Packaging: Advances in technology are enabling the development of smart packaging that has sensors to monitor the condition of the packaged product. This can monitor the temperature, humidity, freshness or condition of food to ensure quality and reduce food waste.

Active packaging: Active packaging are special packaging systems, that have additional functions to improve the shelf life and safety of products. This can include the use of antimicrobial properties, oxygen scavengers, or moisture management to keep the product fresher for longer.

Integrated Information Technology: Packaging could increasingly be integrated with information technology to enable better traceability, authenticity, and consumer interaction. For example, QR codes, NFC tags, or other technologies could be used to provide consumers with additional product information, instructions, or recall notices.

Packaging automation: The automation of packaging processes is expected to increase further to increase efficiency and productivity.

Robots and machines could be used more to speed up packaging operations, reduce errors and improve accuracy.

It should be noted that the development of packaging technologies is also influenced by regulatory frameworks, consumer demands, and economic aspects. The demand for eco-friendly packaging, the pressure to reduce plastic waste, and the trend towards personalized packaging solutions are expected to drive development in this field.

The education system:

The current education system as we know it no longer exists. Why do students sometimes have to carry around up to 10 kg of books and exercise books? In the school system of the future, students will only need a tablet PC.

Some schools have already proven that this is possible with foresight. I also made my contribution in 2000 by introducing a grading system, which was then adopted by the government. The then coordinator, who wanted to keep her classic newspaper-sized paper version from us, was dismissed by the director after protests from me.

In schools of the future, books will no longer be needed, which in turn has a very positive effect on our environment and climate, since the trees that are used for school books are no longer cleared.

There are currently an estimated one billion students in schools worldwide. This number includes students of all ages, from elementary school to secondary school and beyond. If each student only uses one book a year, then you need about 10 million trees just for those books. That's why I don't understand that in times like today when everyone is committed to sustainability and environmental protection, governments don't do much more to promote book-free learning in schools.

Die Digitaltechnik wir auch in Klassenräumen einzug halten.

Personalized Learning: The education system will focus more on individualized learning experiences, taking into account students' unique abilities, learning styles, and interests. Adaptive learning technologies, artificial intelligence and data, analytics will help adapt the learning content and pace to the needs of each individual student.

Classroom of the future.

Blended Learning: Traditional classroom environments are complemented by online and digital learning resources. Blended learning approaches combine face-to-face teaching with virtual platforms, allowing students to access instructional materials anytime, anywhere. This approach promotes flexibility, self-directed learning, and the integration of multimedia resources.

Lifelong learning: The concept of education will go beyond formal schooling. Lifelong learning will be crucial as individuals have to adapt to changing labor markets and societal needs. Ongoing upskilling and reskilling programs will be available for people of all ages to acquire new knowledge and skills throughout their lives.

Emphasis on critical thinking and problem-solving: As automation and artificial intelligence take over routine tasks, the education system will prioritize the development of skills that machines cannot easily reproduce. Critical thinking, creativity, problem-solving, collaboration and adaptability will be key areas of focus to provide students with the skills they need to thrive in a rapidly evolving world.

Lifelong learning.

Global collaboration: Technology will facilitate collaboration between students, educators and experts worldwide. Virtual classrooms and video conferencing tools allow students to gain cross-cultural experiences, work on international projects, and gain a broader perspective on global issues. This networking will promote cultural understanding and global citizenship.

Integration of new technologies: New technologies such as virtual reality (VR), augmented reality (AR), artificial intelligence (AI), and Blockchain will find their way into the education system. These technologies will enhance the learning experience, allowing students to explore immersive environments, simulate real-world scenarios, and receive personalized feedback.

Integration of new technologies.

Focus on Soft Skills and Well being: The future education system recognizes the importance of holistic development and will prioritize the development of soft skills, emotional intelligence and mental well being. Schools will integrate social and emotional learning programs to help students develop resilience, empathy, self-awareness and emotional regulation.

Customizable credentials and competency-based assessment: Traditional assessment systems could evolve into more flexible and inclusive approaches. Student competencies and achievements are assessed using a variety of methods, including project-based assessments, portfolios, and digital badges. Customizable transcripts allow students to demonstrate their unique skills and achievements to potential employers or institutions.

These predictions are speculative and the future education system will likely be shaped by numerous factors that we cannot accurately predict. However, these potential trends offer a glimpse of the direction in which education may be heading in the coming years.

Of course, this requires a lot more energy and electricity.
In the near future, our society's power consumption will increase fivefold. And then we come to the next topic.

Power supply:
The energy supply as we know it today does not work well. Fossil fuels are harmful to the environment. Although nuclear power plants produce a lot of electricity, they also produce a lot of nuclear waste that has to be stored in a controlled manner for a long time. Wind power is not yet mature and, as you can see today, not practicable.
A good solution is power generation with PV, i.e. photovoltaic systems. These solar systems are becoming more and more effective. I could well imagine that soon solar cells will be installed in all roof tiles.
After 50 years of research, there will soon be a breakthrough in the development of fusion reactors with the participation of AI.
For this, however, we still need some modified requirements such as:

Transition to Renewable Energy: There will need to be a sustained shift towards renewable energy sources such as solar, wind, hydro, and geothermal, but not as radical as the government currently intends to implement. At the moment citizens are fighting back because they don't know how to pay the costs and they feel let down by the government. But governments, companies, and individuals will increasingly recognize the importance of reducing carbon emissions and curbing climate change. Advances in renewable energy technologies and falling costs will make them more accessible and economical.

Decentralization and decentralized generation: The future energy landscape could include a more decentralized model, where power generation is distributed among various small-scale renewable energy systems. This can include rooftop solar panels as we see them now, small wind turbines, and community-based energy projects that are then deployed across the board. Local power generation reduces transmission losses, improves grid stability, and gives communities better control over their energy sources.

Advances in Energy Storage: The development of advanced energy storage technologies, such as improved batteries, will play a crucial role in the future energy sector. Energy storage systems enable better integration of intermittent renewable energy sources by storing excess energy and making it available during periods of high demand or low renewable energy production. This will help address the variability and intermittency challenges associated with renewable energy sources.

Smart grids and digitization: The power grid is becoming smarter and more connected through the implementation of smart grid technologies. Advanced sensors, communication systems, and data analysis will enable real-time monitoring, control, and optimization of the network. This improves grid reliability, efficiency, and the integration of renewable energy sources. In addition, digitalization will give consumers better visibility and control over their energy consumption, thereby promoting energy efficiency and demand-response programs.

Electrification of Transportation: The transportation sector will see a significant shift towards electric vehicles (EVs). The increasing adoption of electric vehicles will increase the demand for charging infrastructure and force the energy sector to handle higher electricity loads. This can lead to the development of innovative charging solutions such as fast charging networks and wireless charging technologies.

Energy efficiency and demand-side management: Energy efficiency measures will continue to have priority in the future. Governments, businesses, and individuals will invest in energy-efficient technologies, buildings and industrial processes to reduce energy consumption. Demand-side management strategies, including usage-based pricing, energy-saving incentives, and demand-side management programs, will play a critical role in balancing energy supply and demand.

Integration of artificial intelligence and automation: The energy sector will increasingly use artificial intelligence (AI) and automation to optimize operations, improve energy forecasting and increase system reliability. AI algorithms can analyze large amounts of data to optimize power plant performance, predict maintenance needs, and support grid management decisions. Automation technologies can enable remote monitoring, control and autonomous operation of power plants, improving safety and efficiency.

Carbon Capture, Use, and Storage (CCUS): To reduce greenhouse gas emissions from fossil fuel-based power plants, the use of CCUS technologies could become more widespread. Carbon capture technologies capture CO_2 emissions from power plants and industrial plants and then either store the captured CO_2 underground or use it for other purposes, such as improved oil recovery or the production of synthetic fuels.
These technologies become very important when we come to our next point.

Development of space travel in Earth orbit, the moon, and our solar system:

At some point quite normal.

Space is an exciting and rapidly evolving field with numerous advances on the horizon. While it's difficult to predict the exact future of space travel, here are some possible developments we might see in the near future regarding Earth's orbit, the moon, and the solar system:

Earth Orbit:

Future space station.

Increasing Commercialization: The commercial space industry will continue to grow as more companies enter the market and offer services such as satellite launches, space tourism, and research opportunities. This could result in lower costs, better accessibility and more frequent launches.

Expanding Space Tourism: Space tourism is likely to become more accessible to a wider range of individuals. Companies like SpaceX, Blue Origin, and Virgin Galactic are already working on spacecraft designed to transport tourists to suborbital and orbital destinations.

The future of space tourism.

Satellite constellations: The use of satellite constellations for various purposes, including worldwide internet coverage, will continue to increase. These constellations will provide enhanced connectivity, enable remote sensing capabilities, and support other communications and data services.

In addition, however, a program should also be established by the international community, which will be responsible for collecting garbage and old satellites and feeding them into the recycling cycle.

The Moon:

Lunar Exploration and Exploration: Several space agencies including NASA, ESA, and others have plans for future lunar missions. These missions aim to establish a sustained human presence on the moon, conduct scientific research, and prepare for future human missions to Mars.

A direct launch from Earth to Mars will not be possible because of the use of fossil fuels for the rockets. Therefore it will be necessary that the moon is manned first to mine any necessary resources and materials there.

Permanent lunar base.

Open pit mining on the moon.

Harnessing the Moon's Resources: There is growing interest in harnessing the Moon's resources, such as water ice in permanently shadowed craters, for life support, fuel production, and other uses. The establishment of in situ resource utilization capacities (ISRU) on the moon will serve as a stepping stone to deeper space exploration.

International Cooperation: International cooperation is likely to play an important role in lunar exploration efforts. Initiatives like the Artemis program, which includes partnerships between NASA and international space agencies, aim to facilitate cooperative lunar missions and knowledge sharing.

Solar System Exploration:

Mars Missions and Human Settlement: Mars remains a focus for future human missions. Continued robotic exploration will pave the way for manned missions to Mars, aimed at establishing permanent settlements and conducting scientific research.
Here are some potential developments that could take place in the coming years:

Advances in robotics: Most Mars missions will probably continue to be carried out initially by robots and probes. Future missions could include more advanced robots with enhanced capabilities and autonomy. These robots could be able to perform complex tasks such as sampling, experimentation. and construction.

Human presence: Human missions to Mars could take place in the coming decades. Space agencies like NASA and private companies like SpaceX have plans for human missions to Mars in the future. These missions would bring astronauts to Mars for extended stays, scientific research, and possibly establishing long-term settlements.

This is what bases on the moon might look like.

Technological advances: The development of new technologies will be crucial to enable long-term Mars missions. Advances in space propulsion, life support systems, on-site resource extraction (such as water and oxygen), and radiation protection will play a major role.

Bases must be well protected against radiation.

International cooperation: Mars missions often require the cooperation of several countries and space agencies. In the future, more countries could pool their resources and knowledge to conduct joint Mars missions. International partnerships could accelerate progress and share costs.

Exploring the moons of Mars: In addition to Mars itself, the moons of Mars, called Phobos and Deimos, could also be explored in the future. These moons could serve as way stations to mine resources and test technologies before landing on the Martian surface.

The future of space travel is often difficult to predict as it is influenced by many variable circumstances. Nonetheless, there is considerable interest and commitment to further explore Mars and possibly even establish a future human presence on the Red Planet.

Asteroid mining:
The concept of asteroid mining is gaining traction and offers the potential to extract valuable resources such as metals, water and rare earths from asteroids. This could provide a sustainable source of materials for future space missions and support the development of space infrastructure.

Robotic Probes and Missions: Robotic missions will continue to explore various targets in the solar system, including the moons of Jupiter, the moons of Saturn, and beyond. These missions will deepen our understanding of planetary bodies, search for signs of life and explore the potential for human habitation.
There will also be great potential in sending robots to explore new sources of raw materials on recurring near-Earth meteorites and asteroids.

Autonomous robots work in space.

Advanced Propulsion Technologies: Advances in propulsion technologies such as ion propulsion, nuclear propulsion, and solar sails could revolutionize long-distance spaceflight, enabling faster and more efficient missions to the outer reaches of our solar system. This is necessary because fossil fuel rockets are not effective enough, not fast enough, and can only carry a limited payload.

Robotics for Space: The development of robotics for space is a fascinating field that is constantly advancing. In the future we can expect many potential changes in robotics for space:

Advances in artificial intelligence: As algorithms and AI technologies advance, space robots will be able to perform more complex tasks on their own. They can make adaptive decisions and adapt to new situations, increasing their efficiency and autonomy.

Improvements in robot mobility: Future space robots could have advanced locomotion systems that allow them to move on different surfaces and in different gravitational environments. For example, robots could be able to jump, climb, or levitate on the moon or other celestial bodies.

Miniaturization and modularity: The miniaturization of robots makes it possible to develop compact yet powerful robots for space travel. Modular robots made up of interchangeable components could be able to adapt for specific tasks or missions. This flexibility would allow the robots to be adapted depending on the needs of the mission.

Advanced Sensors and Imaging: Advances in sensor and imaging technology will allow space robots to perceive their surroundings in greater detail. Improved cameras, light detection and ranging (LIDAR) systems, infrared sensors, and other sensors can help robotics map, navigate, and identify resources.

Human-robot collaboration: The future of space robotics is likely to be increasingly characterized by human-robot collaboration. Robots can serve as support for astronauts by taking on dangerous or monotonous tasks. They might also be able to work autonomously with astronauts to solve complex tasks.

These changes in robotics for space travel will expand the possibilities of space exploration and exploitation. They will lead to more efficient missions, improved scientific knowledge, and better use of resources in space.

Unforeseen discoveries and breakthroughs can significantly affect the course of space exploration and travel in the future.

So we only have one question: Are there other civilizations out there in the endless expanses of space?

Conclusions:

Of course, everyone can draw their own conclusions, but I would like to give my summary here.

It is important to note that these are speculations about possible future developments and actual changes may vary based on location, economic development, and technological advances.

Unfortunately, countries, governments, and people have not yet understood that we must protect our planet Earth together instead of killing each other again and again in idiotic wars.

Trillions are repeatedly spent on wars instead of investing in the development of environmentally friendly technologies.

What is also necessary, of course, is that all the inventions that have been developed for the benefit of mankind and then bought up by any company, including OPEC governments, are finally released.

When it comes to our plate, the international common good must come before the personal interests of corporations, greedy hedge funds and governments.

It is up to us humans what kind of future we will have, a bright or a dark one.

www.ingramcontent.com/pod-product-compliance
Lightning Source LLC
Chambersburg PA
CBHW071951210526
45479CB00003B/889